Morning Affirmations

200 Phrases for an Intentional and Openhearted Start to Your Day

Jennifer Williamson

ADAMS MEDIA

NEW YORK   LONDON   TORONTO   SYDNEY   NEW DELHI

Aadamsmedia

Adams Media
An Imprint of Simon & Schuster, Inc.
57 Littlefield Street
Avon, Massachusetts 02322

First Adams Media hardcover edition December 2018

ADAMS MEDIA and colophon are trademarks of Simon & Schuster.

For information about special discounts for bulk purchases, please contact Simon & Schuster Special Sales at 1-866-506-1949 or business@simonandschuster.com.

The Simon & Schuster Speakers Bureau can bring authors to your live event. For more information or to book an event contact the Simon & Schuster Speakers Bureau at 1-866-248-3049 or visit our website at www.simonspeakers.com.

Interior design by Erin Alexander
Interior images © 123RF and Getty Images

Manufactured in the United States of America

10 9 8 7 6 5 4 3 2

Library of Congress Cataloging-in-Publication Data has been applied for.

ISBN 978-1-72140-034-8
ISBN 978-1-72140-035-5 (ebook)

introduction

When the sun rises, so, too, does possibility. Imagine how refreshing it would be to rise each morning with hope, purpose, and joy beating in your heart. The affirmations in this book will help you create this reality by energizing the positive perspectives needed to begin your day right.

Each affirmation here is a training in attention and vision, a conscious consultation of your priorities and the energy you want to surround yourself with. As you trade thoughts like "I don't want to do this day" for thoughts like "I am ready to do my best," you begin to embody the qualities of a brighter reality. You begin embracing your best self and your best life.

The first waking moments of your day promise a chance to begin again, perhaps a little bit better than before—a chance to forge pathways that are not dependent on yesterday or halted by tomorrow. With *Morning Affirmations*, you will be making the most of this golden time to practice the kinds of thought patterns linked with open-mindedness, happiness, and creativity.

You'll soon discover that the trick to rising and shining is no trick at all: just be willing and open to flourishing. Believe in possibility itself. Greet each day with a narrative that serves how you want to experience life. In other words, tell the truths you want to come true. This book is here to serve you.

how to use these affirmations

The thoughts you rely on become the story of how you live and love. Use this book to write your story first thing in the morning, before anyone or anything else does. Use it to positively reinforce what you can control: your energy, your perceptions, your responses, your direction.

Here are some supportive suggestions on making the most of your affirmations so that you can more gracefully wield the light today gives:

- ☉ **Check in with yourself before checking in with the world.** Read your affirmation before reading your emails, watching the news, scouting social media, or responding to outside requests. To promote your undivided attention, go somewhere quiet and inspiring. Play uplifting music to buffer disturbances.

- ☉ **Practice daily.** Affirmations said with repetition and heart can affect reality. Read one affirmation per day, flipping through the book in sequence or at random. Repeat the same affirmation multiple days in a row, if desired.

- ☉ **Read through the affirmation more than once.** Each phrase works like a puzzle, meaning that there is a certain fullness that can be seen only after you have all of the pieces. Read through it again—several times, if desired—to sense its deep resonance.

- **Read slowly.** Meditate on the energy emanating from each sentence. Allow your breathing to slow in time with your reading. Pause with every punctuation mark.

- **Check in with your willingness.** Real and sustainable progress—in your perspective and your patterns—only happens if you are willing. If an affirmation doesn't feel as natural and true as you would like it to, try incorporating the word *willing* or *learning* to make it more fitting. For instance: "I am willing to believe…" or "I am learning how…"

- **Speak emphatically.** Through consistency and conviction, a thought naturally evolves into a thought pattern and then a belief. These words are powerful (and empowering) if you repeat them sincerely enough to absorb their messages. Declare your truths, out loud, on and with purpose. If the thought is too far from your current belief and makes you uneasy, feel free to select another (or apply the previous suggestion).

- **Practice expansive posture.** Sit or stand tall while reading. Afterward, stretch your arms wide and make yourself feel big, literally and figuratively. Stretching makes physical and energetic space within you so you can receive the qualities of the message. This also helps to relieve tension and anxious tendencies.

⊙ **Smile.** Even the hint of a smile harnesses your ability to speak to the greater or innermost part of yourself: the self you are becoming. It is a validation of the affirmation and adds another element of goodwill and hope to the practice. Initially, it might help to close your eyes. Smiling at yourself in the mirror won't feel so alien as it becomes part of your daily ritual.

⊙ **Pair with meditation.** Read an affirmation before or after meditation—find what helps you flow. Visualize the affirmation's essence coming to fruition. Focus on how the message feels in your body, and let the words and imagery turn into pure energy.

⊙ **Crystallize the message.** To help the affirmation root deeper, set up reminders to live into it. Put it in your phone as a notification. Write it down in your planner. Leave notes around your home or office, or tuck one into your pocket or purse, for reaffirmation throughout the day.

Contemplate these affirmations with an open mind. Wake up to your inner light: your power. Rise with intention in your heart and purpose in your bones, and the morning will wake up to something it has not yet seen: you, in all your glorious being.

I am allowed to be new.

I treat today like the dawn of a bright beginning.
I see my reflection like it has just been born
into this brand new morning. Yesterday sleeps.
Tomorrow stays where it is. How sublime it is to
be only here—never having been here before.

When my soul wakes up, it awakens the flowers a busy mind forgets to see. This moment holds treasures just waiting to be discovered. Beautiful things begin blossoming in my present-moment reverence. I begin awakening every lovely thing.

I wake up to this moment.

I am ready to receive what is meant for me.

I welcome every lesson that would support
my soul's progression—even setbacks give way
to comebacks. I am open to this sacred journey
of becoming who I am and unbecoming who
I am not. My path is perfectly my own.

Everything within me is connected to everything around me.

My presence is the spiritual connection I feel to everything. Everything I am now is connected to everything that has yet to be. As I bridge the gap between inside and outside, I start feeling the destination embedded in the journey.

I have a trillion reasons to live.

My hands are for helping and making, my arms for embracing. My feet are for kissing the earth, my legs for discovery. My heart and head co-create with love. Life saturates every cell of my body, celebrating a trillion reasons to live.

I am supported in the process.

It is not my job to control what is not mine to control. I unclench my fists and grant the universe permission to work with me and through me. In this potent space called *the present moment*, I reclaim my power to co-create with faith.

I create a sanctuary within, a place where I rest regardless of what the rest of the world is doing. My light is secured and my peace remains undisturbed. Wherever I go and whatever I do, my inner strength comes with me too.

My core is unshakable.

Peace is my priority.

I don't need to know, have, or do everything
in order for peace to live inside of me. I can
approach anything from a place of inner ease.
I don't chase peace, because it's already here—
seeking me. I just open my heart and let it breathe.

I believe in my ability to figure things out.

My growth is entwined with my positive state of mind. Everything I need is attainable, and I am capable of learning anything I really want to learn. I focus on what I can do from here: I can believe in myself.

I contribute to
a loving world.

I don't need more comfort or resources to leave a loving mark today. I radiate love until the world responds to me. I apply every ounce of desire I have to promote the reality I want to live in. Conscious contribution is my prerogative.

Love leaves nobody out—not even me.
Any reason why I couldn't love myself before
is the reason to love myself now, even more.
The more I love myself, the more I see how
included I always am in love's abiding treaty.

I include myself

in the circle of love.

My body
is a blessing.

I give my body the blessing of respect.
Birth equipped me with this self-healing system
that allows me to breathe, break, repair, and
discover the universe from a unique point
of view. My body is a precious expression
of an otherwise invisible miracle.

I imagine a seamstress of golden light
connecting me to my innermost truth and
I feel a little more whole again. At my core
I am wise and wildly alive. All my wounds,
kissed by the light, are transformed into
guides, gifts, and newfound strength.

Sunshine is

my shaman.

I create a
stress-free reality.

Stress is a response to needs going unmet. This response is a habit—one I can change. In this moment I clear away distraction and greet my needs with compassion. I listen and respond all day long, giving myself some much-needed grace.

I turn tough lessons into blessings.

My experiences are not mistakes. Everything I have gone through has planted something valuable in me or shown me something that I needed to see. I share my insights with care so that they become the blessings that someone else needs to feel.

I honor the struggle that accompanies the strengthening.

It takes awareness and courage to look at my frustration like it's holding a message worth receiving. Today I practice that courageous attention. I am opening my soul to every season and station. I am learning to honor the storms of transformation.

My worth is immeasurable.

Doubt doesn't tell me to stay hidden because that is where I belong; it tells me I have simply forgotten who I am. I am not less than; I am greater than I have ever given myself credit for. Today I remember my worth.

It's fun when fear turns into love.

I play with the idea that fear is here only to bring me closer to love. I use my imagination to rise to what I think I know for sure: on the other side of fear, there is something worth getting excited for.

I practice loving my decisions.

I do not need external validation to prove that I am on the right path. I am as I am on purpose. Today I live from a highly intentional place—in my own way, in my own time, one decision at a time.

I am a powerful force for positive change.

I can change my mindset from lack to abundance, and my energy from striving to thriving. All of my power to change is already ablaze inside of me. My thoughts, words, and actions today reflect my courageous positivity.

I improve with the wisdom that I am already enough.

I can love my way through every change I want to make—this is how I create honest change. I dare myself to love myself enough to enjoy the process. I taste that freedom; I inspire the same in others.

I am free to choose the palette of my emotional sky.

I am the most powerful creator of my reality. I am the artist in charge of designing my internal landscape. I embrace my power to paint the emotions that I want to color my world. This is my liberation.

I am here to be and bring what only I can bring. How I do what I do is my essential contribution—I speak my truth like nobody else can. With each thought I think, I create this offering consciously. I give joyously.

How I live is what I give.

My relationships are platforms for growth.

Instead of dismissing what I do not like or understand, I invite kind conversations about it. If suffering makes an appearance, I stop battling and start asking how we can grow through this. Together, *care-fully*, pain turns into peace.

I need no other reason to love than love.

I do not need to love because I need to be loved.
The love I give is the love I keep. I remove
my conditions for love and love only to *be love*.
Love is always reason enough for loving.

I am not separate from the outcome. I am the whole journey, without beginning or end. Like the seed is filled with everything it needs to grow, my desires are filled with what they need to manifest. Today I travel, blossoming wholeness.

I am the source and the goal.

I shine because I must.

I was born to stand in the light, as a light. I accept my purpose and power to bring hope to the hopeless, love to the unloved and unloving, and peace with a smile. I lead by example: my offerings of light are invitations to shine.

My presence
is my power.

I revel in the magic of taking full, deep breaths.
Graced with my unwavering presence, stress hands
over its power and I regain mine. One breath at
a time, I make this moment my friend. My calm
acceptance weaves peace into my entire life.

*I define my success
by how loving I am.*

I view my journey through the lens of love. I am
willing to love and accept where I am and use
that as a foundation for true fulfillment. My
loving nature is my cause of satisfaction and
the indicator of a day well lived.

I fully embrace the process—the heart of life.

In times of uncertainty I may want clarity and resolution, but what I need first is resilience and depth. What seems like a step backward might actually be a step inward. I step into the process and join life's timeless wholeness.

I trust the timing of my life.

At my own pace, in my own due time, I arrive exactly where I need to be. What I need to know greets me when I am ready. Every experience that's meant for me is, without a doubt, presented to me.

I am open to the mysteries of existence.

I tell my heart that it is okay to be in the dark, for that is where I learn about the light. I remember how to see life through curious eyes and with a mind open to everything I find. It is okay to wonder.

I am curious enough to investigate the wide spectrum of life. My open appreciation is an affirmation of life's endless generosity and intrigue. My mind is alight with imagination. I keep my heart open to receive as much splendor as I can dream.

I lead with curiosity.

Wherever I am, there I am—entirely.

The world needs more people who are vitally alive. I honor the play of shadow and light. I respect the seasons of my ever-evolving life. I am in love with this chance to be alive. Here I am: here, *I am*.

I am mindful of what I am saying to myself about myself. I am mindful of what I am saying to others about others. I tell stories that serve the greatest good. Through empowering tales I water the roots of untellable beauty.

My stories are of service.

Every breath in my lungs is a miracle to me.

Today I look at the earth as though it were magic. I see the planet keeping a lovely little secret in every leaf and blade of grass—even the pebbles too. I breathe deeply, the air wild and sweet with wonder.

Joy is my truth.

Joy speaks my name—it is closer to the truth than anything stress might say. I believe in what brings me into a lighter state of mind. I believe in the place where joy grows like wildflowers. I am learning the language of the heart again.

Now is the time to be easy on myself.

The morning light is a forgiving light. I let it grace my heart and soul. I humbly open my hands to this chance to be at ease and wholly new. I invite the light of forgiveness wherever it's due.

I honor my feelings.

What I am feeling is worthy of being felt.
Through my validation, feelings are allowed
to move and shift. I listen to the calls for
my compassionate awareness and let my
answers be without judgment. Then I can shift.
Transformation is my gift that keeps giving.

I greet this and every moment like it has come to meet *me*. Everything shows up to remind *me* to show up—for this splendid sliver of eternity. My soul is dancing in rhythm with what the universe sends me.

I show up for everything that shows up for me.

I am a helper.

I don't need to be perfect to help; I just
need to be passionate about why I am
helping. I meditate on what I most want
and need to do, and why. My passion for
a better world serves a better world.

Life is an adventure meant to be explored.

I adopt a philosophy that keeps hope alive and makes life worth *really* living. I trade certainty for curiosity. I sense with breathtaking, life-giving awe. I open my gates and let myself live as deeply and richly as I can.

My power is
my responsibility.

Determining my worth and potential is too great a responsibility for anyone else to assume. I brave every fear with a radiant heart. This is the hour that I reconnect with my power. It is time to prioritize what I *can* do.

I discover magic in life's simplicities.

Simplicity births beauty, space, and freedom.
Today I let the little things pull me into their
orbit. I treat the mundane like an element of the
miraculous. I start to see worlds within worlds
and feel the heart of all hearts.

I am the journey.

I am the practitioner and I am the practice.
I am the artist and the masterpiece. I am
made of earth, ocean, and sky. I am allowed
to learn and grow in peace while I walk the
world, heart open and soul wide.

I see only
invitations to shine.

The light of others is not an indicator of my
shadow; it is an invitation for me to discover
my own way to shine. I see reflections of what's
inside of me desiring to be freed. I glow with
all the glory that is uniquely me.

I am open to finding beauty in unlikely places.

Serendipity is like finding a gift in the middle of nowhere with my name on it. I leave extra space for the unknown today. I plan for beauty through my schedule—still open enough for a surprisingly beautiful *something* to find me.

My heart is recovering its childlike wonder. My eyes remember how to discover. I am willing to see just how joyous life can be. I am willing to treat any given moment today like another opportunity to play. I decide to be free.

I play because that, too, is love.

My dawn has come.

I arise like a butterfly that has just broken free
from its cocoon. I emerge like the lotus, pure
and untouched by yesterday's hurt. My soul is
flowering with the birth of this new morning.
A new day is dawning. I am looking up.

The way I treat others is dependent on my truth, not theirs—this is how powerful I am. No matter what happens "out there," I am steady in my essence. Nothing can take away who I am.

I treat people based on who I am.

I use every "I am" wisely today.

If I catch an unhelpful "I am" escaping my lips, I declare my willingness to change the script. Any heavy story, old or new, can be lightened with a bolder view. I choose to use speech that empowers my being. I create wisely.

My trust tells a story of abundance.

I am learning the language of trust, which always gives more than it takes. I am ready to experience a miracle, so I give thanks for abundance until I start to see that it's who I am. Miracles are part of the plan.

My direction matters.

I am exactly where I need to be to get to where I want to be. To get anywhere, I start here. One "yes" at a time, one "no" at a time, I head in the direction that makes my soul feel at home *right here*.

I rest in serenity while the world spins.

I soften the edges of my perception and find harmony within the disharmony. I know there is a center where I can go, where stillness braves the storm. Today I belong to the core of the world: its light and airy soul.

I brighten the world by trusting that there is still light to be seen—and then I become a light. I accept my power and let it radiate from the inside out. Turbulent seas cannot stop me from being a beacon of hope for the world.

I am a lighthouse.

Love is how I heal.

I move with care. I consume gratitude. I think and speak warmly. I confront illness with visions of wellness. I treat discomfort with compassion. I weave loving-kindness into every decision, creating an atmosphere in which my cells can function well. This is how I heal.

I am the beauty
I decide to become.

I am willing to see the truth about myself,
no matter how beautiful or not beautiful
it is. There are precious gifts that only I
can give; they are just waiting for me to
release the jaded beliefs that have kept
them hidden. I let myself bloom.

I elicit everyday magic to help me stretch time, heighten my senses, and deepen my adoration. I adopt a curious heart so that I can feel with wonder. I practice a grateful perspective so that I can see with pleasure. Life is a magnificent sea—full of treasure.

I am hunting for treasure.

I am the change.

The change I want to see is alive within me. I
think about solutions and possibilities. I start
to see things differently and the universe
reorganizes its energy accordingly. My flame
of passion kindles change and action. I start
lighting up the world around me.

I flow in the stream of well-being.

I can tune into life's abundant source of wisdom whenever I choose. To flow, I resist nothing. I take nothing for granted. I align my energy with everything uplifting and true. I am guided and connected, supported and protected, fluid and free.

I am on purpose.

I live life on my own terms, according to my own
timeline, aligned with my values, in the direction
of my desires—on purpose. I make my passion
and my presence the most marvelous things
about me. My brilliance is mine alone to reveal.

I am divinely aware.

I welcome all the colors, textures, tastes, sounds, scents, and sights—every signature of life. I see symmetry and synchronicity. I hear the faintest whispers of the cosmos. I feel for life's pulse in the air. I move consciously and breathe deeply— thoroughly, wondrously, divinely aware.

I am in vibrational harmony with the whole universe.

I focus on feeling guided, supported, and connected to a presence greater than my ego. I release the burden of judging who and where I am. I am energy walking the earth, a spiritual being communing with the universe.

Compassion is my medicine of choice.

Today I treat pain with compassion, not more pain. It is deceptively easy to judge but more fulfilling to love. I look deeper than the surface hurt and see a core wound. Responding to something unloving with love makes me feel free.

I am the beginning and the fulfillment of my core desires. I access my infinite core of wisdom in the silence of the morning. I awaken this energy of attraction within, harnessing its power to bring my desires—and my potential—to fruition.

My true self is unbounded.

I have no problems, only experiences.

I can practice stillness even in the middle of what might be perceived as a problem. I can greet turbulence with an open heart and heartbreak with full presence. I see the sacredness even in pain. I am wholly alive, whatever this moment contains.

I allow myself to feel with every cell of my being. I touch the preciousness and glory of life. I hide from nothing; I am totally available and not afraid to feel. In every luminous, waking moment, I linger a few beats longer.

I feel the pulse of this moment.

There is room for everything under the sun.

I leave space for everything: for what I don't know and for the evolution of what I do know. I am discerning and forgiving. I am grateful and enthusiastic. I explore every experience like it holds something for growth or for letting go.

My thoughts are powerful.

The thoughts I bring to life shape the way I experience life. As I step into my power as a creative being, reality proves itself malleable. I focus my thoughts and energy on the kind of world I wish existed. The future is listening.

I manifest my desires with ease and harmony.

I tap into the powerful feeling force of life itself. My desire sprouts from the intelligence of nature. My actions spring from a deep-seated peace. I attract all the nourishment and guidance available to me and move toward the life that's waiting for me.

I am an extension of something bountiful and bright.

I join the intimate dance of life. My heart beats in time with the entire universe and all of its creations. I am awake to the spectacular gift of existence. What pleasure my soul takes in this grand new day.

If I am ever in an unloving situation, I ask how I could better love and then generate the courage to answer lovingly. I make my responses conscious. I am never stuck in any belief that makes me feel anything less than loved and loving.

I let love reign.

I change for peace.

I am allowed to change as many times as
I need to for peace. I am not limited to one
way of walking this earth. I meet the winds of
change with a river of peace flowing through
my veins. I am alight with possibility.

I take this day
as "just" one day.

Today is a gift that was never a guarantee. I
align my thinking with the splendor of being
alive—here, breathing, glimpsing what an
awesome miracle *I* am. I live the only way the
universe intends: one day at a time.

I flow in the current.

I savor, without clinging to the seasons of my life.
I bask in a fluid experience, flowing from one
moment to the next, not forcing but rejoicing. I feel
endings melting into beginnings. I am lightened
like a breeze, right in the middle of everything.

I am life, indefinitely.

I am remarkable—an expression and
extension of the energy coursing through
every cell and soul. I am not the limitation that
others might have me believe in. There
is more to me than the five senses reveal.
It is astounding really, my being here.

I choose narratives that reflect how I *want* to feel and what I *can* do. My potential is limited by nothing. There is no end to what is possible for me—nothing I cannot do, nothing I cannot be.

My soul is free to explore any reality it pleases.

My perspective is flexible.

I am not stuck in a stale frame of mind. I am receptive to a perspective that has yet to grace me with its light. My willingness to see things differently saves me from the paralysis of perfection. I am always opening and polishing.

I see miracles everywhere.

I sense the intelligence that springs from quiet trees
and fluttering wings. I sense that I am swimming
in an endless sea of miracles just waiting to be
discovered. The "little" things keep calling to me.
A miracle is a miracle no matter its span or size.

I take care of my responses.

I can respond to stress and heartache with a greater reverence for life. My responses are mine to care for, my gifts to the greater good, mine alone to control. Through my tender loving echoes, I lighten the weight of the world.

Today is an exploration of who I am and who I am not, of what I love and want to experience more of. I am a soul walking back home to its true nature. Every experience teaches me how to be more like myself.

I am walking home.

I trust my direction.

I hold dear what matters to me but remain
flexible in the ways I walk this journey. I practice
surrendering every "should" and "should have." I
can appreciate where I am and honor where I've
been and still accomplish what needs to be done.

I am connected to the powerful, constant, universal force that is creation. I send out vibrations that speak the same language as what I desire. I attract more of who I am. I believe in what is coming to me—and then let the universe respond creatively.

I attract all that I need.

Gratitude is the way I give and receive.

My appreciation is to abundance like the sun is to a flower: as I shine on what I adore, I watch its petals unfold to reveal something more. I dig deeper today to find the seed of what I can be grateful for.

I live the entirety of this day, without delay.

I let go of the unimportant. I waste no energy today on what distracts me from living vibrantly, and remain committed to what I care about most deeply. I *do not* squander my time on earth. I *do* live fully on purpose.

I bask in this morning with its new light.

This waking moment is my life, containing every possibility and memory of the heart. Thank you, Mother Earth and Universe, for kissing me again with your light. Me and this morning: I let this be enough, for it is everything.

My spirit is at play.

Today is an exploration. I see challenges as opportunities to show up in new ways. I turn mundane tasks into adventures and games. I wonder about what I can discover. My curiosity seeks to uncover the buried treasure and hidden pleasure in everything.

I promote what I love.

I make what I am inspired to make. I follow and leave only love in my wake. My choices reflect my hopes today. Staying true to what I love sends an invitation to others. I radiate my truth and invite.

I am moving toward what I want.

My hopes, desires, and ambitions make me human—part of life's natural rhythm. Today I nurture my authenticity, celebrate where I am going, and let my fulfillments flow outward to benefit others. I am gathering the means to make my dreams a reality.

I vow to love.

Yesterday is asleep and tomorrow is a dream.
Today I give the world the best of me. If I can
give just a little, I give wholeheartedly. Even a
little is a lot when love leads—and love is that
"little" thing the world needs.

My forgiveness lightens me.

Forgiveness returns me to the light that wants to fill the cracks in my armor. I forgive so that I can go deeper into the life that *I* am meant to live. I allow space to be made inside. I breathe until I breathe only light.

Today I tell myself what I need to hear: I am who I need. I am already everything I believe the title, money, person, or thing will make me. I am a flowering tree, in sync with my ripening authenticity.

I am already everything I need.

I am always on time.

Time and space prevent everything from happening to me all at once. I cannot be anywhere I am not meant to be. I am learning the secret to being in the right place at the right time: knowing I always am.

Through my energy and attention, I propel this morning's emerging intention and see it all the way through to its manifestation. What I focus on flowers. I let my focused awareness grow expansive, too, gathering support for what I wish to come true.

I am always creating my world

I live lightly
on the earth.

There are many ways to make my love for Mother Earth tangible today. I explore my own grateful presence, for which she so generously provides a platform. I nourish her soul and she nourishes mine. I think and walk lightly, matching her ways.

I am a survivor.

I can survive impossible things—I've done
that before. I keep learning how to be better,
not bitter, and to work with my past, not
against it. Today I wear my scars to show
how a phoenix is born from ashes and hope.

I find fortitude
in my vulnerability.

My honest, open heart feels more deeply and
broadly than a heart that is closed by what it
knows. My authenticity is life-enriching. My truth
is its own defense and my ultimate strength. I
live openly so that I may *truly* live.

I learn how to see with new eyes.

I am never too experienced or lost to see life again for the very first time. I open my eyes once more and rise with a renewed heart. Like the dawn, I remake the world, this time a little bit brighter.

Whatever comes my way today, I can breathe my way through it. I start right now: breathing light and space down into my belly, my rib cage expanding in every direction. Conscious breathing is my freedom— through it my uncaged heart can sing.

I breathe through every emotion.

I am worthy of living
a life worth loving.

My life is a gift meant for living. My gifts are
uniquely mine for the giving. This morning is a
fresh chance to give like I haven't given before—
to live and to love like it's what I am meant for.

My positive energy leads the way.

I accept reality as it is, while throwing something wonderful into the mix: the energy by which I choose to live. Positive thinking brightens my brain and helps me succeed. Today I focus on solutions and seeds of possibility. Optimism is how I cooperate.

I praise this morning because *this* is where peace and change can take place—not back then and not "someday, when." How I show up today is up to me. Every decision I make reflects who I am choosing to be.

I am strong in who I choose to be.

I am whole,
without conditions.

I arise from the realm of wholeness: home to my soul. There is nothing missing inside of me. I can see myself in everything around me. Whatever I do today, it is enough. And so am I. And so it is.

My attention sends an extraordinary message.

Today I make everyone feel seen in the strength of my presence. I create space for sharing and real connection. By engaging with each moment, I make myself available to others: I hear stories and see hearts. I am interesting because I am *interested*.

My mind is beautiful.

I beautify my mind with compassion and honesty. I try acceptance and patience with whatever I find. I let thoughts come and go with greater ease, watering the flowers and gently pulling up the weeds. Even when it rains, I rejoice in what my garden gains.

All is well,
all in due time.

Each morning I am given enough light for
the day. I take what I have been given,
palms and heart open wide. My life is a
masterpiece, arranged one piece at a time,
a poem I can read only line by line.

I dream above my circumstances.

I face my current reality with visions of a brighter future. I let the past and present guide and drive what I feel in my heart is right. I connect my desire to the people, practices, and beliefs that enliven this emerging reality.

I am radiant inside and out.

I let go of the need to control what goes on inside of others and focus on growing what is beautiful inside of me. What I cultivate within can spread hope all over. As my roots grow deeper, my wings stretch out.

I enter this morning with a heart ready to receive—and I am ready to respect my needs. I awaken the smallest moments that feel nourishing. Mere seconds become gateways to a greater life of devotion. I practice filling my own cup.

My simple self-care is radical love.

I trust this season to deepen my aliveness.

The wretched and the divine: I get both in this lifetime and sometimes not one without the other. Life is everything. I do not avoid what life has to offer. Today I live as boldly and breathtakingly wholly as I can.

In the still clarity of this morning, I envision my best and truest self. I imagine harmonizing my inner and outer worlds—blending thought with movement. I delight in *how* I do what I do and use each moment to commune with my dreams.

I pursue my best life.

Perfection is in my progression.

Nothing needs to be perfect for me to set positive change in motion; it *mustn't* be. My soul is wedded to the universe's endless curiosity and generosity. Today is for the continuation of my inward journey. I walk toward what feels most truthful to me.

I am awake to life.

I consciously slide into the rhythms of this day, awake to every subtle detail that meets me here. I am aware of every thought, breath, and moment. I awaken the energies that were once dormant—they wake up to me because *I* have awakened.

My heart is my guide.

I give my head permission to stop fighting
for answers. I drop into the valley of my heart
instead. I ask my heart questions and listen for
the whispers from within. Force dissolves into
feeling. Wisdom is rising and I go where I am led.

I belong to myself.

I am my own planet with my own atmosphere, orbit, and gravitational pull. I am shamelessly my own, steady and true even when I stand alone. At every intersection, no matter the place, I remember that I belong to myself first. I hold my own space.

Life is my classroom and I am teachable.
Like the sun, I renew my earthly devotion
to growth. Life does not demand that I
know everything; it urges me to stay open
to everything—priceless lessons and the
remembrance of who I am.

I am a student of life.

Good things are happening on my behalf.

The universe is always working on behalf of the greatest good of all. I am humble in the face of anything the universe sends me. I trust that whatever is happening to me is also happening *for* me. Through my openness, I receive.

I release my grip on the outcome.

I may not see the big picture yet. The outcome may not reflect my plans. I rest in the certainty that life's powerful current will carry me through. I go with this masterly plan. One experience at a time, my story is unfolding.

I give away love like it's what I am made of.

I lift others through my gentle gaze and caring touch, through my attitude and expressions of love. I give the world around me what's evergreen inside of me. The more I love, the easier it becomes to live.

I appeal to life's treasury.

I am joined to a rich network of radiant life energy: abundance as a source. I relish this state of prosperity and joy, and dip my toes in its endless ocean. I awaken earthly and ethereal treasures—abundance itself is seeking me.

I can control what I focus on, so I focus on what I can control. I strengthen the feelings that I want to last; I tell myself only things that I want to come true. Life elevates what I pay attention to.

I pay attention to
what I want to grow.

I seek validation from my own heart.

I reaffirm my heart's brilliance—shining unclouded by anyone else's judgment. I feel the difference between proving myself to others and doing what is best for me. When it comes to outside opinions and requests, I answer "yes" only when my heart says "YES!"

I honor the light within.

My heart is my altar and guide, my body a temple of life. Today I respect the essential light that every soul houses. The stars in me come forth to greet the stars in every living, breathing galaxy. My inner light bows to the light in others.

I do more than survive.

I pay attention to more than just making it through this day. I feed my own flourishing. I dive into the depths of each precious experience that makes up life. I invite total fulfillment and profound connection—wherever I am. Bottomless *being* comes through, come what may.

I am always doing the best that I can with the clarity and resources I have. My personal best is subject to its own evolution. I show up today, willing to explore my next level of excellence. I experiment with new solutions. I improve with acceptance.

My best is enough.

My body is my friend.

My body is listening to me, absorbing every energy, spoken or unspoken. I am the life breathing through this instrument of expression. The morning new, I teach my body an important lesson: it is a companion on this earthly voyage, the vessel carrying me home.

I am here to experience how life can be experienced. I am here to express what can be expressed. I am living, breathing proof that the universe longs to know itself better. My purpose is in my heartbeat. With my hand on my heart, I remember.

Life is the point.

My soul is still.

Deep within the core of me, there is a quiet knowing that all will be well. The slate has been cleared again so that today truly becomes new. The words *I am grateful* rise through me like early morning glories. I bloom and move from a place of peace.

I am one with life.

I wonder how deeply my soul has been woven into the fabric of conscious life. I imagine that everyone is my brother, my sister—a child. I picture life-sustaining roots fusing since the dawn of time. I am entwined with everything under the blessed sun.

I celebrate life's wealth of possibilities.

I am ever expanding yet whole, wise enough to know that there is plenty left to learn, and rich with what it takes to grow. I seek out rubies in the rubble, humbled by the unknown. Little by little I practice my own priceless unfolding.

Beauty is rising again.

Pain is a stimulus that sends me searching for who I am meant to be. I may change, but I am never diminished. I can rise from destruction, better than before; this is what beautiful feels like. I feel my perennial heart rising once more.

I can handle every season of my life.

I am an example of what's possible after the fall. In the cold of winter, my heart whispers the memory of spring. If it feels impossible to keep going, I breathe and take just one step at a time. I remember how resilient I can be.

I play with new ways of seeing.

I dip into my infinite reservoir of pure awareness.
I am sincerely and completely awake. I do not
judge whatever I see today—I seek only to see
with a relaxed curiosity. I am the conscious
master of how I see what I see.

I am learning the ways of love.

Love has many names and today I reacquaint myself with them. Grace, kindness, cooperation, gratitude, patience, and peace are just a few ways in which I practice loving my way through this day. My conscious thoughts and actions express the love I'm exploring inside.

Life is constantly giving to me.

Life does not merely happen to me; it happens to support me. I am the master creator of what I choose to do with what has been given. The way I relate to what comes my way determines the energy I live in.

I use brief moments of respite during my day to stretch time by bringing in space. Deep inhales deliver ease. Long exhales spark freedom. Seconds is enough time to reset my system and replenish my existence. No matter what, I keep my being spacious.

I embrace every moment of space.

Morning is music
to my soul.

I embrace this moment. Never have I heard it before; never will I hear it again. Every sound, soft and loud, is composing a melody. I get quieter. I hear the voice of love like a breeze as the rising sun wakes the world again.

I listen to the wisdom of my soul without needing to document it for anyone else. I listen to the stories of others before, or even without, needing to formulate a reply. I listen because I am interested in another depth of life.

I listen just to listen.

I am a powerful agent for my own healing.

Wounds are for healing and today I *am* that healing presence. I am not defined by circumstance. I am no victim. I am not imprisoned by opinion or memory. Today my growth is a softening; it is fertile ground for something new.

I am worthy of all things wonderful.

I welcome all the ways the universe might bless me. I acknowledge the good that is already in my life. I radiate gratitude and delight. I draw that which is good into *my* goodness. I write it on my heart: wonder is unfolding.

I am essentially enough.

My worth is something I brought into this world with me. It cannot be measured by productivity or calculated by awards received. I am the seed that already contains all the wisdom it needs to grow. I am the universe learning how to breathe. I am enough—always.

I am strong in my comebacks.

If I fall, I am allowed to rise—more swiftly and
gracefully than I did last time. I experiment with
my ability to reorganize my energy in any given
moment. I see in hardship a chance for deeper
fulfillment. I take pride in rising.

I release the frantic energy of the ego: the constricting need to make decisions swiftly. I summon guidance from above and within before I commit to anything. I breathe freedom into my body. I focus on feeling good. I trust the timing of my intuitive answers.

I welcome inspired ideas.

I am a peace activist.

Through the way I live, I give love a voice. I do not fight or force; I radiate peace and let those who resonate come to me. Peace is the first and last choice I make today. Peace *is* my way.

*Letting go
is a lightness.*

For just this moment I drop my agenda and expectations. I accept the morning's invitation to not be too in control—not too full of habit, plans, details, or tomorrow. I am called to infuse inspiration and spontaneity into today. Life is precious.

I grow through discomfort.

I do not run away from, numb, or resist what already is. I build courage and compassion in the face of uncertainty. From this place of acceptance, transformation begins. I can move and make a friend out of anything.

I am able and willing to change. My flexible awareness sustains my success. I am not stuck in preconceptions about how my life is supposed to manifest. I release biases and receive the gifts of change. I allow *myself* to become a gift of change.

I am infinitely adaptable.

I am an expression of truth.

I am ready to forgive myself for believing anything my inner critic has said. I trade the stories in my head for something new: a belief that doesn't dim my truth. I journey toward a brighter reality—a fuller expression of my light.

On the horizon of my gratitude lie unspoken thanks: blessings yet to be born. Being grateful for what I have is a powerful way to expand. Today I generate prosperity by focusing on the blessings already here. Full of love and thanks, I am a magnet for boundless joy.

My gratitude orchestrates joy.

I release the darkness.

I am ready to accept all the difficult moments
of my past—so that I can set everything free.
I do the same with my worries. I let go of the
night. What is mine to keep pours through the
honeyed stillness of the morning.

I find joy with others.

I lift the veil of separateness and go beyond the boundaries I see. Closing the gap, I feel the bliss of unity—the fulfillment of others feels like my own. Every thought, word, and action of mine contributes to the freedom and happiness of all.

I am practicing peace.

If I can remain calm in the stillness, I can learn
to remain calm in the flow. I have survived
everything so far; I trust in the power that
carries me forward. I am Peace in training.
Every moment of inner stillness is a victory.

I rejoice in how far I have come. In this new season I live in the breath; I feel my heart beating; I answer to my soul. I am not my limitation; I am my greatest freedom. This time around, I soar.

I open a new chapter of my soul.

My life gets sweeter when I share it.

My authentic self is meant to be shared
with kindred hearts and fellow souls. Sharing
is a power that brings miracles. I vow to share
my purpose today. This is how I expand
the energy of love for everyone.

I am on a
wonderful adventure.

Even what doesn't feel wonderful is working
secretly in my favor. The circle of life has
met me here to help me be and see who and
what is best for me. Life is never stuck and
neither am I. I decide to explore.

I can be a blessing for many.

I am guided to what is best for every sentient being living alongside me. My compassion is all-inclusive. I use my strengths to serve the greater good in ways that feel good to me. I participate in the manifestation of countless blessings.

The opinions and behaviors of others are reflections of who *they* are. I free myself from their weight; they are not mine to carry. I keep my light and stream it to all who need it. I live from within.

I am a channel for the light inside of me.

Being alive is the special occasion.

I get to experience how it feels to be alive:
the purpose underlying every purpose in life.
I release any resistance to basking in the
glory of existing. Each breath is a gift to me,
a messenger of the miracle it is to *be*.

I seek intrinsically rewarding experiences.

I order my day so that I am furthering my purpose. I am deeply connected to what my soul came here to do. I focus on what I can give rather than what I can get, living in a way that brings meaning to my life.

Fear does not stop me today from doing what is right. I interrupt fear with the courage to love. I walk toward the kind of fear that leads to expansion and growth; I walk away from the fear that is not serving me anymore.

Fear guides me forward.

I am an alchemist.

I am capable of transforming negative
experiences into opportunities to love. I rewrite
my grievances, turning suffering into something
productive. I overturn the ordinary and uncover
the hidden gems tucked inside. There is so much
room on earth to bring magic to life.

I grow through what I go through.

Winds blow fiercely not to uproot my life; their power serves my own. I am learning to say "thank you" to everything—for lessons in sight and revelations of my own might. I am growing into who I most need myself to be.

My mind is a vast open sky.

I immerse myself in the moment, just as it is—wherever I am today. I have a wide-open awareness of every sensation. I practice pure experience without layers of story or opinion. I am the sky watching clouds of thought pass by.

My happiness is in each step.

Happiness is a devotional practice and I am worthy of its fruits. I plant and harvest crops of happiness today through loving-kindness and gratitude, in my relationships and work, and by bringing meaning to what I do. I find that happiness is a journey too.

I flow forward.

I merge with the essence of what I desire most—
like the beginning of a path is connected to
wherever it goes. I set my intentions, vow to do
my best, and then let them go. My energy is my
current. I allow effortless creation to unfold.

I discover a whole new way of being in the world.

I can perceive the world any way that I choose. I can pause often just to notice how stunning life can be. It is up to me to decide how I give and receive, let go, and breathe.

I don't wait for the world to give me a reason to shine. My light gives others permission to shine. I don't hesitate to make the world around me beautiful. I am a proactive seeker: I lead with the energy I seek.

I model what I want to see.

Letting go of fear is my assignment here.

I let go of the fear that I should be somewhere or someone else. I release self-deprecating stories and old ways of finding false security. I am not afraid of being wrong or misunderstood. I lighten every burdensome reason to fear.

My suffering was necessary for growth,
yet it is only a slice of my life—and a part is
never greater than the whole. There remains
something beautiful contained within: this circle
houses everything. My openness to all of life
elevates my soul. I can still smile.

Life is still beautiful.

This moment is my life.

I move more deeply and quietly this morning.
The energy underneath the noise and movement
asks only for me to join it. I do not will this
moment to be something that it's not. I inhale
what is, receiving everything this life has to give.

I inhabit my experiences fully.

I entertain the sweet simplicity of doing one thing at a time. I infuse space in between activities. I allow mental habits of busyness to unravel. I practice a new, fruitful habit: contentment of *being*. With less clutter in my mind, I am more alive.

I shine like the sun.

I am the caretaker of my energy, the composer
of my vibration. Like the sun, I radiate my
authentic nature without getting pulled into
every story. I see the whole world with luminous
eyes. I influence others by how I rise.

I reserve space for joy.

Instead of calling today work, I realize it is play.
Instead of trying to arrive, I jump into the journey.
My perfection is not required. My enthusiasm is
rewarded. I am passionate and patient. I make it
through every obstacle without losing my flame.

I am in sync with the natural world.

I am one with the force that creates the rhythms and cycles of nature. I fall more deeply into this season, studying its patient and powerful ways. I make my way back to the wholeness from which I came.

I wake up to my worthiness without needing any reason at all. I most love the parts of me that need love the most right now. I treat my body like a friend—and so it is. I finally accept my innate goodness.

I strip my value of question marks.

Life is abloom.

True wealth is in my ability to perceive each
moment for what it's worth. I place happiness
in front of success and the whole earth rejoices.
My simple wonder retrieves the bliss obscured
by plain sight. I value the infinite blessings of
meaningful connection—everywhere, there's light.

I am radiant with life.

In a world captivated by past and future, my presence is a powerful spectacle—a celebration of life. From this sacred space I attract more radiance into my life. I rise this morning, strong and bright, passionately aware. I am committed to being here.

I have come to write my energetic signature on the earth. I rejoice in my discoveries and allow my soul to play. Mysteries do not discourage me—there is ample room in the cosmos. I wear a light heart today.

I am a cosmic soul exploring the world.

I advocate for myself.

I speak up lovingly and ask for what I need
to feel whole and well. I stand my sacred
ground and hold on to my peace. I am gentle
with myself yet firm in my expression of what
is right for me. I step forward, fully.

My happiness

ripens over time.

I don't need permission to make happiness
a direction. My destination is in each step. I
bring joy with me along the way so that I may
enjoy its fruits upon my arrival. True happiness
reflects the path I am walking.

I am congruent with my values.

The behavior of others does not diminish my
goodness. I can honor my beliefs in a way
that does not disrespect the beliefs of others.
Patience is my charity. I cannot be swayed from
the light and goodwill I have to give.

My desires matter.

I am continuously gaining clarity about how I want to live. My experiences are integral to the expansion of what I love. I honor how I truly want to feel in my skin. It becomes easier to say "no" to what doesn't serve where I am going.

My spirit is unbroken.

I discover wisdom rising from the crevices where the light got in, like wildflowers springing forth through cracked cement. I am a piece of art mended with gold. I am a patchwork quilt woven with hope. I am clothed in my own brand of brilliance.

I plant seeds of kindness.

As I sew compassion into my words, I sow happiness in my relationships. I reach out with deep awareness and appreciation. Empathy gives me the wisdom I need to seed fields of greater love. I am a healer and a light of the world.

I am surrounded by people to love, which
sometimes means to forgive. My aches
seek a healing that only mercy can give.
I organize something fruitful and cleansing:
loving how *I* choose to live today. This is
the soul medicine that I take.

I employ the alchemy
of forgiveness.

I believe in the magic

of starting anew.

I adopt a carefree state of awareness with no ego demands. I am at ease with not knowing and open to new ideas. Wrapped in the golden dawn of another chance, I am willing to begin again.

What I wish to see more of in the world is
mirroring what I can give. My service feels
light like love because that is what
I am made of. I honor what fills my cup
so that I can serve like the sun.

I have come to give.

There is plenty for everyone, including me.

I trust in the circular nature of change. If I miss something, its essence is bound to come back around again. I believe in my own creative and resilient nature. I trade discouragement for excitement and the whole universe expands with me.

I stay true to myself.

I am ready to be heard and seen, understood and loved, for who I really am. There is power in my vulnerability and a chance for real connection. No more masks; it is time to bare my soul. It is time to get back home.

I believe in my dreams.

Not everyone needs to believe in my dreams, but *I do*. I believe beyond what I can see. I feel the fruition of my desires as if I were already living them. I am a visionary. I believe in *me*. My possibilities have no end.

*I trust my
intuitive cues.*

My intuition is my powerful companion and
the gateway to inspired living. Every whisper
from within is an inkling of truth that I listen
to. I awaken and strengthen my sacred
insight—synchronicity and harmony begin to
flood my life. My wisdom is my lifeline.

My trust is a fruitful practice.

There is a force greater than me handling life in its entirety; my faith rests here. I let the universe reveal itself through me without demanding that it reveal its secrets to me. I enjoy the sweet anticipation of whatever is on its way.

I choose the beliefs, rituals, and relationships
that nurture my deepest peace and joy.
I am not waiting to live my own definition
of success. I am alive with a genuine interest
in being here—as I intend to be.

*I prioritize the way
I want to live.*

My sunlit spirit is my gift.

I can extract meaning from anything when I bring joy with me. My internal glow is eternally satisfying. I sprout seeds of hope and harmony by sharing my sunlight with others. I pursue my intention to brighten every room and conversation.

I can change
my mind

I am allowed to believe in something that feels better. I open the windows of my mind and let some fresh air find its way in. My acceptance combined with my fluid state of mind sparks greater freedom and potential. I was born to change.

Every experience shows me the way back to the light. Every person is teaching me how to trust my inner guide. Everything that I am meant to experience arrives according to my soul's readiness—not a moment sooner or later than it should.

Everything contributes to my becoming.

I include everyone in my plans for love.

I create with love today and do so in an all-inclusive way—making room for everyone in my loving awareness. From the inside out I perpetuate love on this planet. My grand agenda for the day is pure and revolutionary love.

I embrace the

beautiful messes.

Life is transition—not straight lines or
smoothness but storms and adaptation and
wild flow. I dance into beautiful chaos with my
loving intention. I am totally allowed to dream
and play before things fall into place. Beauty
can be made from just about anything.

I am radically responsible for who I am.

Sometimes enlightened, at times enraged, I am a human graced with the divine responsibility of making this world a better place. The past and future alike benefit from my unwavering presence. I am here with a mission to serve.

about the author

JENNIFER WILLIAMSON is the creator of the online journal AimHappy.com, where she explores conscious living after loss through healing poetry, affirmation, and down-to-earth wisdom. Her first book, *Sleep Affirmations*, marked the beginning of a dream come true: making her work and love tangible in the world. Every composition is an offering of light and an invitation to shine. She lives in central Massachusetts.

Miracles happen in the morning.

I believe in miracles because I can see them
in every alchemical process—from the ever-
changing season to the dawning day. Miracles
are in every beginning. I follow the whispers
of renewal. I stand at the threshold of a new
perception: certainly, it is a miracle.